The Majesty of
THE HORSE

DEAN SERVER

SMITHMARK

This edition published in 1997 by
SMITHMARK Publishers,
a division of U.S. Media Holdings, Inc.,
115 West 18th Street, New York, NY 10011

SMITHMARK books are available for bulk
purchase for sales promotion and premium use.
For details write or call the manager of special sales,
SMITHMARK Publishers,
115 West 18th Street, New York, NY 10011

This book was designed and produced by
Todtri Productions Limited
P.O. Box 572, New York, NY 10116-0572
FAX: (212) 279-1241

Printed and bound in Singapore

Library of Congress Catalog Card Number 97-066062

ISBN 0-7651-9244-6

Author: Dean Server

Publisher: Robert M. Tod
Editorial Director: Elizabeth Loonan
Book Designer: Mark Weinberg
Senior Editor: Cynthia Sternau
Project Editor: Ann Kirby
Photo Editor: Edward Douglas
Picture Researchers: Meiers Tambeau, Laura Wyss
Production Coordinator: Jay Weiser
Desktop Associate: Paul Kachur
Typesetting: Command-O Design

Picture Credits

Art Resource, New York
Albertina, Vienna 67
Bridgeman Art Library 29, 52, 84–85
Chateau Malmaison/Giraudon 71
Free Library of Philadelphia/Scala 33
Kunsthalle, Hamburg/Bridgeman 74
Erich Lessing 14, 34–35, 76–77
The Louvre, Paris 30–31, 79
Musée des Beaux-Arts, Tourcoing, France 23
Musée Bonnat, Bayonne, France/Giraudon 39
Musée Carnavalet, Paris 50–51
Musée d'Orsay, Paris 76–77
National Gallery, Prague/Werner Forman Archive 6
Palazzo Publico, Siena 87
Scala 33
Schloss Ambras, Innsbruck 14
The Tate Gallery, London 5, 16

FPG International
L.O.L. Inc. 18–19, 26, 56–57

Bob Langrish
10, 12, 13, 15, 20, 21, 22, 28 (top & bottom), 36, 40–41, 42, 43, 45, 48, 52,
54, 55, 58, 59, 64 (top), 66, 68, 69, 70, 72–73, 78, 80, 82, 86 (top & bottom), 90, 91, 92, 93, 94, 95, 96, 97, 98, 99, 100, 101, 102, 103, 104–105, 106
(left), 106–107, 108, 109, 110 (left), 110–111, 112, 113, 114, 115, 116, 117,
118, 119, 122, 123, 124, 125

The Picture Cube
Jerry Koontz 47–48, 62–63
Inga Spence 37

Picture Perfect
8–9, 24–25, 27, 32, 60, 61, 65, 75, 81, 83, 88–89, 120–121, 126–127

Tom Stack & Associates
S.K. Patrick 64 (bottom)
Inga Spence 38

CONTENTS

INTRODUCTION

Remnants of the earliest ancestor of the horse of the present day, known as *Eohippus*, or the Dawn Horse, have been found in North America. Paleontologists have traced these fossils to the Eocene epoch, somewhere between forty million and sixty million years ago. During the Ice Ages that followed, the Eohippus and its descendants utilized the land bridges which then connected the continents to spread into Asia and Europe.

For uncertain reasons, the horse vanished from North America approximately ten thousand years ago, at the end of the Pleistocene epoch, not to return until Spanish conquistadors brought horses with them from Europe in the sixteenth century. Researchers have speculated that disease may have wiped out the North American horse; or perhaps the growth in human population forced them to move away, or their numbers were greatly reduced through hunting. The submergence of the land bridges between the continents ended any chance of horses returning to their land of origin.

The creature that the present-day horse evolved from bore little resemblance to its current descendants. It was much smaller than even the tiniest pony of today, standing at less than 2 feet (60 centimeters) tall, or 4 to 5 hands (a hand, at 4 inches, or approximately 10 centimeters, is the universal standard for measuring a horse's height). The Eohippus did not have a single hoof on each foot but rather four toes on the front feet and three on the back feet. Its teeth were different, not designed for grazing but rather for its diet of shrubs and tree branches. Also, the size of the brain was smaller, the skull less flexible, and the eyes set differently, providing less peripheral vision.

As Eohippus evolved, the size of the species increased, its legs becoming much longer and the entire body generally more flexible. Through the succeeding epochs, the feet of the horse evolved as living conditions changed. After about ten million years, the four toes of the Eohippus had become three toes in its descendant, the much larger *Mesohippus*. After several million years more of evolution, no longer did the species walk flat-footed—it balanced itself on its toes. A further descendant, the *Miohippus*, began eventually to walk on a central toe. At last, the *Pliohippus*, the first single-hoofed descendant of the Eohippus, emerged about six million years ago. While the horse's feet were evolving, so were its teeth, which became stronger, larger, and longer—and better able to pull up and chew grass, which had become the staple of its diet.

Approximately two million years ago, *Equus*, the descendant of the Pliohippus and the genus of all future equines, first appeared. About ten thousand years ago, after the horse had become extinct in North and South America, four distinct breeds developed in Asia and Europe. The Asian Wild Horse, now also known as Przewalski's Horse, and the small and fast Tarpan from eastern Europe are thought to be the ancestral sources for today's so-called "hot-blooded" breeds, such as the Arabian and the Thoroughbred. In northern Europe, the much larger Forest Horse was the ancestor of the powerful working horses of today. These breeds, known as "cold-bloods," include the

Shoeing, a portrayal of a horse being shod, was executed in 1844 by the English animal painter Sir Edwin Landseer, who was very popular in his day. The horse is likely kept docile by the presence of its stable pets, a dog and a mule.

春風得意 悲鴻想像盛世
戊子冬日北平寄中

Twentieth-century artist Hsu Pei-Hung enjoyed drawing horses in his primitive works, including *Grazing Horses,* from 1948.

Shire and the Clydesdale. Another northern breed also developed, known as the Tundra Horse. Its remains have been discovered in northeast Siberia, though its influence on present-day horses is less certain.

History

Initially, horses were hunted as a food source. It is unclear when horses were first tamed and domesticated, though the date is thought to be at least as distant as 2000 B.C. It is likely that domesticated horses were originally raised for their meat and their milk. Fighting Nomads of eastern Europe and Asia may have been the first to employ horses in war. The Hyksos, conquerors of Egypt in 1715 B.C., introduced the horse-drawn chariot into combat. Soon after, the armies of Greece utilized the chariot. The horse's primary use for more than three thousand years as a vehicle for war had been firmly established.

The development of the saddle allowed riders a much greater opportunity to utilize the speed and maneuvering ability of a horse. By the ninth century B.C., the Scythian tribes rode horses into battle from their home base near the Black Sea, and invaders from Mongolia rode their horses to conquests in China and India. Huns, Avars, and Magyars also made successful invasions into Europe on horseback.

Following the middle ages many other uses for horses were developed. In the eighteenth century, the horse began to be worked extensively on farms, replacing the slower ox. Ponies, which were small enough to fit into mines, were used to carry coal. Larger breeds were able to carry logs out of forests and to haul many different kinds of cargo. In addition, horses were used to control herds of livestock on farms and ranches.

As roads were cleared and carriage construction improved, the horse-drawn coach became the primary means of transportation throughout Europe. By the middle of the nineteenth century, stagecoaches played a major part in the settlement of the American West.

The horse has inhabited almost all parts of the world for centuries, adapting to a variety of climates and conditions. Whether bred for power or speed, raised in cold or hot climates, or controlled from a saddle or a carriage, the importance and usefulness of this extraordinary creature has long been acknowledged. Yet other qualities of its character—its shapeliness and beauty, its grace—have resulted in the horse's being celebrated the world over. While other species such as the camel and the ox have fulfilled many of the same functions, few other animals have developed the romance and the lore that the horse has.

FOLLOWING PAGE:
"In God's wildness lies the hope of the world—the great fresh unblighted, unredeemed wilderness."
—JOHN MUIR,
Alaska Fragment

CHAPTER ONE

THE LANGUAGE OF HORSES

The gestation period of a horse is eleven months. Planned equine matings are thus arranged for a mare to foal at an optimum date. Most horses in the western hemisphere are given a universal birthday of May 1, but for industry convenience racing horses are given a universal birthday of January 1. In the southern hemisphere, the date is August 1. Even though all racehorses are given the same birthday, breeders usually don't try to have their mares foal at the earliest recognized date. In the northern hemisphere's cold climates, January and February foals do not have immediate access to the fertile grasses of spring, nor do their mothers, from whom they are nursing. As a result, such foals are disadvantaged as compared to spring foals.

Life Cycle

More than one foal is unusual for a horse. Twin foals rarely survive, and if they do, are usually noticeably smaller than a single foal. Following birth, after a short struggle, a new foal is normally able to stand on its long legs within a half hour, and it begins nursing shortly thereafter. Within two months, with its teeth appearing, the new foal is able to eat solid foods. By half a year, it will be weaned from its mother. At about this time the foal will have a full set of baby teeth, known as "milk" teeth. As the weanling grows into a yearling, the horse becomes less leggy and moves around easier, though it is not yet completely coordinated. The major bones of the legs of a yearling are not developed enough for it to withstand any work or heavy training; the horse will not be ready for such tasks until it is at least two years old. For ponies, maturity is even slower. Some cannot perform until age five.

Horses usually reach sexual maturity after two years, though most are not bred until after the third year and usually later. This explains the difficulty of translating horse age into human age. If age three or four in a horse corresponds to human adolescence, a human's age would be four or five times that of a horse. But many stallions and mares are still producing offspring past the age of twenty, and some breeds live past the age of thirty. Thus the 4–1 or 5–1 human/horse age ratio does not compute.

It is well known that a horse's age can be determined by looking at its teeth. But this is only possible until a horse is about ten years old. Up to that point, age can be told by counting the number of teeth and noting their stage of development. After age ten, the teeth begin to lose their sharpness from both use and aging. A horse's hair can also change as it gets older. Grays and Roans lose their dark hairs and become almost totally white. A horse's legs become less sturdy as it gets older, and it is much less capable of performing the athletic tasks it could handle in its youth. The older horse is, of

Admired for its grace and the beauty of its distinctive gray coat, the ancient and influential Arabian is one of the most popular and valuable of all breeds.

Though the number of wild horses has diminished, many herds still roam what open spaces remain around the world, including these in the Caucasus Mountains in southeastern Europe.

Winter climate does not bother most horses, as is evident in this idyllic setting. Some breeds are able to thrive in cold weather because they possess very long nasal passages, which warm the air they breathe.

course, more susceptible to illness and degeneration, and as it ages it clearly requires more attention to stay healthy.

Food and Shelter

A horse's stall in its stable needs to be at least 10 x 10 feet (3 x 3 meters), covered by about a foot (30 centimeters) of bedding. Ideal material for a horse's bedding includes sawdust, straw, and wood shavings. This material needs to be replaced daily, as horses are susceptible to disease from bacteria, especially in their hooves. In most stables, each horse is assigned a groom, who cleans the stall, changes the bedding, fills the food box, and also bathes, cleans, and combs the horse. There are special brushes used for combing different parts of the horse, including one for the main body and another for the tail.

A horse's diet consists of grass, grain, and hay. In its stall, or within reach of it, a supply of hay is kept, usually in a rack; grain is contained in a box called a manger. Vitamins, minerals,

and other supplements are added to the diet. A horse will eat as much as 14 pounds (6.5 kilograms) of hay a day, as well as up to 12 quarts (11.5 liters) of oats. Most horses will drink more than 10 gallons (38 liters) of water every day.

Types and Breeds

In the last two thousand years, three intermingled influences were dominant in the development of the lighter equine breeds. These were the Arabian Horse, which spread out from the deserts of the Middle East; the Barb, which came from northern Africa and was imported into Europe through Spain; and the Spanish Horse, which descended from the Barb but evolved into a specific and very influential breed.

There were no horses in Arabia two thousand years ago. Camels, which were known for their speed, were then the primary means of transportation. It is not clear where the horses that were imported to Arabia came from, though the most likely sources were Syria, Mesopotamia,

Gundakar Fürst Dietrichstein.

and North Africa. The Arabian desert would not seem the proper environment for a grazing animal to prosper, but the Arabian horse did. The importance of the Arabian was greatly expanded by the Muslim Empire's expansion, beginning in the seventh century. The breed went into India, Asia Minor, China, and Europe. The Arabian remains a major breed today, and its influence is felt most significantly through its descendant, the Thoroughbred.

Researchers believe that the Barb breed was derived from wild, ancient horses. Eventually, they may have been mixed with Arabian blood, but the Barb maintained a distinctive appearance. The Islamic army, which invaded Spain in the seventh century, brought the Barb with them, and the Barb and its descendants then became quite an influential breed throughout Europe.

The descendants of the Arabian and the Barb are examples of hot-blooded breeds. These are horses usually best suited, or at least originally developed, in warm or hot

climates. They are normally capable of being ridden under saddle or carrying a harness, though they cannot carry loads of great size. They are also generally known for their speed, though not necessarily lacking in strength or stamina.

North African horses were first brought into Spain at approximately 400 B.C. They were crossed with the smaller local breeds, producing the original Spanish Horse which became the dominant breed in Europe for many centuries, where its descendants include the Andalusian and the Lipizzaner. The Spanish's importation to North America by conquistadors led to the development of many more important breeds, including the Mustang and the Appaloosa.

Foals of domesticated mares, such as the young Welsh Pony seen here with its dam, will stay with their mothers for about six months. At that point, the foal will have a set of baby teeth and will be capable of chewing and digesting solid foods.

In the royal courts of Europe, both riders and horses wore ornaments for special occasions. This seventeenth-century painting depicts a prince who performed in a horse ballet commemorating the marriage of Austrian Emperor Leopold I. *Prince Dietrichstein* by Jan Thomas.

As horses were transported to different environments, they were endangered by attack from predators, a threat always faced by wild horses. This danger was depicted by George Stubbs in *Horse Attacked By a Lion* (1769).

Gray or roan horses usually have dark hairs mixed with white in their coats. As a horse ages, however, most of the dark hairs disappear and an older gray will often be all white.

Larger breeds which developed in Europe and other northern climates are known as cold-blooded breeds. They are much heavier and sturdier than hot-bloods, weighing more than 1400 pounds (670 kilograms), with some weighing well over a ton (950 kilograms). They do not have nearly as much speed as lighter breeds and are almost never ridden under saddle, but they do have greater working capacities. Historically, their strength has been utilized both for domestic and military activities. Also referred to as draft horses, most of the cold-blooded breeds descend from the ancient, extinct Forest Horse, the huge equine that had adapted to the climates of northern Europe. The Forest Horse had a different conformation than hot-blooded breeds, with much thicker bone and muscle mass and larger hooves. It also had a different diet, being less reliant on grass for its food. In addition to the Forest Horse, some heavy breeds may be descendants of the ancient Siberian Tundra Horse, another large breed resistant to cold.

Some heavy breeds were crossed with the blood of lighter breeds, usually descendants of the Spanish Horse, to give them better movement and physical refinement. Other breeds which are not just influenced but are direct descendants of both hot- and cold-blooded breeds are referred to as warm-blooded. These include such breeds as the Quarter Horse and those horses descending from the Spanish Horse, including the Pinto and the Appaloosa.

The other distinct group of the horse world is the Pony, differentiated specifically by its height—actually, in fact, its lack of height. While full-size breeds are normally 15 hands or higher, all Ponies are less than 15 hands, with some smaller than 10 hands. Most Ponies are categorized as warm-bloods, though there are cold- and hot-blooded breeds as well.

Conformation

The conformation, or physical structure, of horses varies depending on the size and purpose of a breed. Years of selective breeding following epochs of evolution have produced proper conformation for each breed. The legs

"Grow old along with me!
The best is yet to be,
The last of life, for which
the first was made.
Our times are in his hand."
—ROBERT BROWNING,
Rabbi Ben Ezra

The natural exuberance and jumping ability of the horse is evident as this gray frolics through a field on a Maryland farm.

of a Thoroughbred, for example, are longer and thinner than most breeds and generate a more rapid gallop. Draft horses, bred to carry heavy burdens or perform arduous tasks, have much thicker and shorter legs, which do not generate much speed but produce high levels of power. Ponies have proportionately shorter legs than the larger hot-blooded breeds. They are also thicker through the body, though their backs are usually much shorter.

Many of the terms used to described the physique of a horse are unique; others are more familiar. Cannon bones, on the front legs below the shoulders, arms, and knees, are similar to human shin bones. (The term "bucked shins" refers to a young horse not yet perfectly coordinated whose shins have become inflamed from excessive use of under-developed bones.) Ideal cannon bones will be straight from the knees down, and any variation can cause physical problems. The term "over at the knee" refers to a horse whose knees bend forward above the cannon bones, while "back at the knee," a more serious condition, de-scribes a horse whose knees lean backward above the cannon bones, a condition which can put a dangerous amount of stress on the legs during activity.

Further down the leg, the cannon bones connect into the fetlock joint. This area of the leg is supported by the weight-bearing sesamoid, a bone which is one of the most often injured in serious breakdowns. Below the fetlocks are the bones called the pasterns which extend into the hoof, or, more correctly, into the coffin bone inside the hoof. The hoof is not the equivalent of the human foot but rather the human toe. A horse normally balances itself on its toe, or hoof, and that is why when a horse is standing or walking slowly the fetlocks remain elevated above the hooves. When a horse picks up speed, the hooves push into the ground hard enough for the pasterns to flex down, bringing the fetlocks close to the ground.

The withers is the portion of the horse where its neck and back are joined. In most breeds, though not in all, the neck elevates from this location. The withers is the point from where a horse's height is measured. So if a horse is listed at 16 hands, or 64 inches (1.6 meters), the top of the horse's head may actually be a great deal higher depending on the angle of the neck.

A horse's shoulder connects to the rest of the body through muscle, not bone, as in humans. The back and midsection, or girth, of a horse varies greatly depending on the breed. The length of the horse's back determines what size individual can ride, or if the horse can be ridden at all. Ponies, lacking in height, tend to have girths that are thicker and wider proportionately than larger horses, which have longer legs.

The muscles around the top of the horse's tail are called the hindquarters, and they can become heavily muscled. A rippled appearance of these muscles is usually the sign of a very fit horse. The joint at the top of a horse's back leg is known as the stifle (a horse who has injured this joint is described as having "grabbed a stifle"). The stifle then connects to the tibia, which then connects to the hock, which is similar to a human ankle bone. Below the hocks, the cannon bones, pasterns, and hooves are structured similarly to those of the front legs.

Many of the uses for working horses have been eliminated by automation, and their numbers are no longer so plentiful. Yet the descendants of the large and powerful breeds, such as these Percherons, are beloved by their owners for their courage and beauty.

Pleasure riding by women increased in
the nineteenth century. In *On a horse:
Mademoiselle Croizette in Riding Costume,*
by Charles Emile Carolus-Duran, the rider's
long, flowing skirt precluded riding astride.

The stride of a horse has been measured
at about 25 to 30 feet (8 to 9 meters),
which is approximately three times the
length of its body. In order to accomplish
this, a galloping horse needs to be air-
borne temporarily, as seen in this photo.

Colors

In more superstitious times, certain horse colors were thought to be good or bad luck, though the theories varied in different countries. In Spain, black horses were thought to bring good luck, but in France they were thought to be unlucky. In pagan times, white horses were considered descendants of the fire-breathing stallions who pulled the chariots of the gods across the sky. In some cultures, white horses were often sacrificed as a gesture to the god of the sun.

Today, one of the reasons for the popularity of the horse is its wide array of colors. Certain breeds are known specifically for a color or color pattern. A good example of this is the Palomino, with its distinctive gold coat. Others are the Appaloosa, famous for its varying spots, and the Pinto, whose colors have a splashed-on appearance. Many other breeds have distinctive though not unusual coloring. The Suffolk Punch, for example, consistently has a chestnut roan coat. The large Percheron is noted for its gray colors, as are Arabians. The mixing of breeds has produced many color combinations and has established standards in new breeds.

The basic colors of current breeds are bay, black, brown, chestnut, gray, and roan. There are many combinations and shades of colors, such as a blue roan—a white coat with some black hair which gives off a blue tint—and a light bay, which is a bay with some chestnut coloring. At young ages in certain breeds, it is not easy to differentiate colors. Dark bay is hard to distinguish from brown and differentiating a gray (white with black hairs) from a roan (white with chestnut) is sometimes difficult. In the Thoroughbred breed, so many mistakes have been made in the past that all such horses are now classified as "gray or roan."

A mixing of colors sometimes produces a predictable color, sometimes not. For instance, a mating of two chestnuts will always produce a chestnut, though this does not happen with all colors. The great Thoroughbred Secretariat, for

"The sun's rim dips,
   the stars rush out:
At one stride comes
   the dark;
With far-heard
   whisper o'er the sea
Off shot the specter
   bark."
   —SAMUEL TAYLOR COLERIDGE,
   The Eolian Harp

"Now the great winds
   shoreward blow;
Now the salt tides
   seaward flow;
Now the wild horses
   play,
Champ and chafe and
   toss in the spray."
   —MATTHEW ARNOLD,
   The Forsaken Merman

On a typical horse farm, mares and their foals are allowed to roam together. But each stallion is separated and, when outdoors, allowed to roam freely only in its own paddock.

There are several distinctive markings and colorings possible on each horse, especially about the face. A horse with a "white face," as seen here, is white in color from the ears down to the muzzle.

example, was a chestnut, though both of his parents were bays. Coloring within a breed can also change over time. Early in the twentieth century, grays were rare among Thoroughbreds, but they are quite a bit more common now, thanks mostly to the influence of a very prolific and successful gray sire, Mahmoud. Colors in other breeds have changed over time as well, most of them through the colorful patterns of the influential Spanish Horse, ancestor of the Appaloosa, the Palomino, and the Pinto.

Facial markings distinguish horses as well. A small white spot between the eyes is called a star. A similarly small mark around the nose is called a snip. A narrow strip of white down the face is called a stripe, while a wider strip is known as a blaze. When the entire area from below the ears down is white, this is called a white face. All these patterns are well known and make identification of an individual horse much easier. White markings on the feet and legs are quite common. Traditionally, there have been horsemen who do not want horses with more than one white foot, since this supposedly leads to physical problems (though this seems to be superstition).

The calm, pastoral setting often evident in paintings of country riding is apparent in *Over the Fence* by Alfredo Tominz. The horses and riders exist in an isolated world which consists only of green grass and blue skies.

Gaits

There are a number of different gaits utilized by horses, including the specialized strides of such breeds as the American Saddlebred and the Tennessee Walking Horse. But among most other breeds there are five main gaits: the walk, the canter, the trot, the gallop, and the amble. All of these gaits have their own particular patterns. In certain types of racing and dressage, it is a vital requirement that a horse's stride follow certain standards.

Naturally, the slowest of the gaits is the walk, though for purposes of dressage competition there are several different speeds of the walk. These are called medium, collected, extended, and free, and each walk varies the length and elevation of the stride. In the basic walk of most breeds, a back leg touches first, and if it is the left hind leg, it is followed by the left front leg, then right hind, and finally the right front. The sides are reversed if the right hind leg touches first.

A more complicated stride is the canter, which has a three-beat pace. The horse will land first on its right front leg, then its left hind and right foreleg stride simultaneously, followed by the left front to finish the stride. That is the pattern when a horse is on a left "lead" (so-called, even though the left front leg is the last to hit the ground). For a right lead, the sides are reversed. The canter is used when a horse is making a circle.

The natural trotting gait of a horse is a two-part stride. The front left and the rear right legs stride in unison, as do the front right and rear left legs. Though not nearly as fast as a full gallop, horses in competition running on the trot can reach speeds as high as 35 miles (about 55 kilometers) an hour.

Another gait used in competition is the amble, or, as the high-speed amble is known, the pace. In this stride, the two legs of one side stride in unison. Running alternately on the left

This eighteen-century painting portrays an English viscount with his mare, Maria. Notice her right hind leg oddly aloft, and the strange look of her tail. *Asheton, First Viscount Curzon, and his Mare Maria* by George Stubbs.

"When tillage begins, other arts
follow. The farmers therefore are
the founders of human civilization."

—DANIEL WEBSTER, *On Agriculture*

and right sides, pacers are occasionally called sidewheelers. Pacers, unlike almost all trotters, frequently wear hobbles, leg equipment designed to help them maintain their stride. The hobbles loop around the legs and pull with the left or right strides. Though not considered a natural gait, most horses who race on the pace find it much easier to stay on their gait in competition, whereas trotters quite frequently do not (off-gaited horses are described as going "off stride," or "breaking stride," or just going "on a break"). Pacers run somewhat faster than trotters, running a mile (1.6 kilometers) about three seconds faster than a comparable trotter.

Though at times the gallop may appear to be a free-wheeling, undisciplined motion, it actually follows a clear pattern. On a right lead, the left hind leg lands first, followed by the right hind, then the left foreleg, followed by the right foreleg. A horse on a left lead would reverse sides. Horses will frequently change leads when on the gallop, much as a human switches sides after hopping too long on one leg. Horses in competition, running around a track circumference, will usually change leads going into and out of turns. On a counterclockwise, or left-turning track, it is preferred that horses run on a right lead in straightaways and a left lead on the turns. These leads would be reversed on a clockwise, or right-turning, course.

The depiction of horses in many quaint, rural settings by Currier & Ives helped to popularize the image of the horse in nineteenth-century America. *Preparing for Market* by Currier & Ives.

Horses have been
a subject for artists
from prehistoric
times to the present.
The eighteenth-
century English
naturalist George
Stubbs frequently
used horses as a sub-
ject for his paintings,
including this work,
Mares and Foals.

Shoes

The sensitive hoof of a horse requires frequent attention, and the horse shoe, like the human shoe, provides support and protection. It is necessary to change a horse's shoes over time because the hooves are constantly growing. When old shoes are removed, the excessive growth on the hoof must be trimmed away. Different parts of the hoof grow at different rates. If the horse's feet are not properly cared for, the growth of the hoof may be irregular and can lead to physical problems. This is a problem for many private horse owners today because it is now much more difficult to find a good blacksmith, or farrier, than it was in the nineteenth century, when horses were much more common in the major cities.

When shoeing a horse, the farrier must take precautions by wearing a protective covering over the legs known as chaps. Since they must hold the horse's legs at awkward angles, farriers are in constant danger of being given a powerful and dangerous kick, possibly while holding sharp objects in their hands, including nails. Chaps are usually made of a heavy

leather and they greatly decrease the chance of injury. Some horses that are very difficult to control during shoeing cannot be worked on unless they are temporarily tied down.

After precautions are taken, the process of getting the bare foot ready for a new shoe begins by cleaning off the hoof and removing dead skin. The excessive growth of the hoof is then removed through steps referred to as "paring" and "rasping." Paring involves a wrenchlike tool which pinches out the excess skin. Rasping is done with a longer, straighter tool which resembles and works similarly to a long file.

After smoothing the foot flat and level, the shoe is then applied, though it must first be shaped to fit the foot. Nails are then driven through the shoe into the hoof until the shoe is secured. An alternate approach to applying shoes has also been developed. In this method,

The development of America's West would have been far different without the horse. Even today, the horse is an essential part of most ranches in the western United States. Here two ranch hands are trying to capture wild Mustangs.

The Lipizanner is one of the most popular of all show horses, attracting large crowds around the world. Though usually performing under saddle, as seen in this photo, the Lipizanner can also perform in harness.

the shoe is bonded to the hoof rather than nailed in. The premise for this practice is that any nail driven into a horse's hoof weakens the hoof, and eventually lessens the horse's capabilities. Nailing on shoes, however, is still the much more common practice.

Different breeds wear different types of shoes. Racing horses wear shoes made of as light a material as possible; when an injury to the hoof forces the horse to wear heavier shoes for its protection, its performance usually

suffers. Different types of cleats are an important feature of horseshoes. These can provide better traction for a horse running through wet grounds, climbing mountains, or traveling through snowy terrain. There are also specialized shoes for certain breeds, most notably the American Saddlebred and the Tennessee Walking Horse, which wear shoes more heavily weighted toward the toe. This helps them perform certain high-stepping maneuvers in the show ring by elevating their stride.

FOLLOWING PAGE:
The tradition of the
fox hunt continues
with or without the
fox. The pleasures
of a horseback ride
through the country-
side remain popular
—for instance, here
among England's
lush green acres.

The most celebrated
horse of mythology was
the winged Pegasus, the
offspring of Poseidon and
the faithful companion
of Bellerophon. Pegasus
was further immortalized
in this work by Peter
Paul Rubens, *Bellerophon
On Pegasus, Slaying the
Chimera,* which portrays
the famous Greek legend.

Horses in show rings often employ
spectacular gaits or, as seen in this
picture, display specialized training.
The riders here are officers of the
Cadre Noir, the French Cavalry School.

Though the practical need for horses in most
official capacities no longer exists, many countries maintain the tradition of mounted horses
for certain public events. This is particularly
true in England, and can be observed here in
this display of mounted drummers at Windsor.

Saddles, Bridles, and Bits

The invention of the saddle in the early Christian era made it much more practical to ride and control a horse. Saddles originally were carved from a wooden base, as are many saddles today, which also utilize leather, rawhide, and other strong materials. A saddle must provide enough comfort for long rides, while maintaining durability and sturdiness. Through the centuries, improvements such as straps, padding, and stirrups have been added. The western saddle used by American cowboys included a horn behind the seat to which the cowboy could tie his rope, or lariat. Usually a blanket was put over the back of the horse before the saddle was tied on, though on more modern saddles a softer pad, often made of sheepskin, is used.

Different saddles are built depending on the purpose of the rider. Jumping saddles are designed to keep the rider well forward, because in conventional saddles the leap of the horse will knock the rider back toward the hindquarters. Saddles designed for racing other than jumping have less padding, are built much flatter, and are quite a bit lighter. Dressage saddles allow the rider to sit more upright in order to perform the various requirements of competition.

Bridles are used to control a horse's movement through the maneuvering of straps, or reins. The bridle fits around the horse's head. After it is secured, the rider grips the reins and can steer the direction of the horse, rouse it to move faster, or pull the reins back to stop the horse. There are several bridle designs, the most basic being the snaffle bridle, which applies limited pressure to the horse. The double bridle has more reins, allowing the experienced rider more control over the horse. Another variation is the western bridle, in which only one end of each rein is attached.

The bit is a mouthpiece which is attached to the bridle. Movements of the reins are felt in the mouth and provide a quick response. Originally, bits were shaped from the bones of other animals. Today, most are made of flexible metal, though many are constructed of softer material to provide more comfort.

Traditionally, the American circus brought in exotic animals from Africa as a main attraction, but they also commonly utilized horses. This Ringling Brothers and Barnum & Bailey poster depicts teams of horses in the style of ancient chariots.

The ears of a horse are often an indication of its mood. When they stand up, like those of the gray in this picture, it is an indication that the horse is alert and attentive.

"O for a life
of sensations
rather than
of thoughts!"
—JOHN KEATS

CHAPTER TWO

HORSES IN MOTION

The history of horse-drawn carriages reaches back nearly four thousand years. Carriages were initially used in warfare with much smaller carts, or chariots, pulled by two or four horses. The speeds possible with the chariot gave enormous advantage to its operators. Early chariots had two wheels over a floor which was attached to a semicircle guard. Originally, when a driver had four horses pulling the chariot, he held separate reins for each pair or even for each horse. Later improvements allowed for one set of reins to control all four horses.

Chariots, Carriages, and Wagons

After the Hyksos used the chariot to conquer Egypt in 1715 B.C., the Egyptians themselves—as well as the Greeks and Chinese—employed the chariot in subsequent centuries. The Chinese made great advancements in chariot equipment, inventing the shaft and collar which were used to control teams of horses. It wasn't until much later, when the development of the saddle made horseback riding easier, that the chariot became less a tool of war.

Both the ancient Greeks and Romans used the chariot for transportation and as a part of large processions. By the middle ages, the horse-drawn vehicle had become much more sophisticated. An important breakthrough in carriage design was made by Hungarian craftsmen. The coach they designed had larger wheels on the back than in front, and this allowed for safer and easier turning. In subsequent centuries, further engineering advances in design and construction allowed the pulling power of the horse to be increased. Carriages were then able to carry passengers and freight over difficult terrain.

As more roads were cleared and transportation increased, the stagecoach began to operate regularly in England early in the eighteenth century. It provided public transportation and was also used to deliver mail. The coaches traveled for as much as eighteen hours a day, with teams of horses changed at specified locations. An English stagecoach could carry as many as fourteen passengers and could cover as much as 40 miles (65 kilometers) in a day.

In America, stagecoaches were used in the nineteenth century to cover the vast distances of the largely unsettled western regions of the nation. The most common American stagecoach was the Concord, which was made of high quality wood, weighed about 2,500 pounds (1,200 kilograms), and cost about one thousand dollars. The Concord was constructed with specially designed braces to absorb the shocks of rough ground. It seated nine inside the coach, and more on top of the vehicle. The trip from St. Louis to California took about a month, covering an average of 60 to 70 miles (95 to 110 kilometers) each day.

The Arabian bloodlines are maintained meticulously by the World Arabian Horse Organization. Arabians are now bred throughout the world and fetch high prices at public auctions.

In *The Walk Along
the Champs Élysées*
Jean Beraud portrays
an era in Paris that
is lost forever. Indi-
vidual horse carriages
became popular in
the late nineteenth
century and were
common until the ad-
vent of the automobile.

When enough roads were cleared in England, new advances in carriage technology allowed for unprecedented transportation and mail delivery. *The Exeter Royal Mail on a Country Road* by James Pollard.

Less fancy covered wagons were used in the American West of the nineteenth century too, usually by individual families settling the region. Traveling long distances from eastern America, settlers required wagons which were strong and sturdy but not too heavy. Otherwise, of course, the wagon could not be pulled for long distances by a team of horses. It was not unusual for families to be stranded along the western routes after excessive loads in their wagons resulted in their horses breaking down.

Technological improvements continued in large horse-drawn carriages well into the nineteenth century until the steam engines of boats and locomotives began to eliminate their need. But after 1850, the private use of carriages expanded greatly throughout Europe and America. Fancy carts like the Barouche or the Spider Phaeton were the rage of the late nineteenth century. Some carriages were designed for pairs, others for single horses. Some were designed for pleasure riding, while others were needed for basic transportation. There were a number of less sporting carriages as well, which were built for various industries. Horse-drawn wagons carrying such items as beer, milk, and garbage became common sights in major metropolitan cities late in the nineteenth century and well into the twentieth century.

After the automobile became widespread, the necessity for local businesses and private citizens to operate horse-drawn carriages all but disappeared. Yet the pleasure of a comfortable ride through a park or countryside while being pulled along by one horse or a team of horses remains, and is to this day a popular leisure activity.

Since the middle ages, horses have been a part of most festivals and parades throughout Europe. These days, many ancient uses for horses are reenacted at carnivals or fairs. Here a team of horses pulls an outmoded carriage at a public event in Aachen, Germany, in 1990.

Working Horses

The horse was a virtually indispensable part of the world's military forces from ancient times through World War I. Both the speed and maneuverability offered by lighter breeds and the power of heavy breeds were effectively utilized. In most countries, cavalry officers were considered the elite of all soldiers. The cavalry was still very important for several countries in World War II, most notably Russia, which deployed over a million horses. The advent of automatic weapons and dependable tanks in the twentieth century lessened the need for horses in the military, and the United States eliminated its cavalry wing after World War II.

Though most nations of the world have abolished the horse from their armies except for ceremonial purposes, local governments still make great use of horses in police work, particularly in large cities. Police horses perform many urban tasks and are extremely useful in the control of large crowds. Because they are often in the midst of a lot of people and noise, police horses need to have an easy-going nature. They cannot be too high-strung,

FOLLOWING PAGE:
"Time, like an ever-rolling stream, bears all its sons away; they fly forgotten, as a dream dies at the opening day."
—ISAAC WATTS, *Psalm*

One or two horses attached to a wagon is most common. A more specialized arrangement is that of three horses pulling a carriage, known as a troika, seen here at the Moscow Hippodrome.

"From the desert
I come to thee
On a stallion shod
withe fire,
And the winds are
left behind
In the speed of
my desire."
—BAYARD TAYLOR,
Bedouin Song

which is why Thoroughbreds are a rarity in police work.

Perhaps the most famous of all police horses are those ridden by the Royal Canadian Mounted Police. Originally known as the Northwest Mounted Police when they were founded in 1873, the "Mounties" policed the sprawling, open territories of Canada's northwest on horseback in their distinctive helmets and red coats. They were renamed the Royal Canadian Mounted Police in 1920, and are considered the equivalent of the United States' FBI. The Mounties travel mostly by automobile now, however, and their horses are used only in ceremonial activities.

Draft horses have been used to transport most types of industrial cargo. As the locomotive and the steamboat expanded settlements in the nineteenth century, especially in western America, more horses were needed to meet the great increase in agricultural production. Horses working in huge teams were used to sow crops and, eventually, to harvest them. There was also an increased demand for horses to haul materials into and out of an ever expanding number of rail yards and boat docks.

Horse-drawn carriages not only transported people throughout Europe beginning in the eighteenth century, they also delivered mail on their journeys. In the United States stagecoaches performed the same functions, but because of the size of the carriages the horses could not travel at fast speeds. In 1860, a new service was created in the midwestern state of Missouri. Called the Pony Express, it cut down the time of delivery from Missouri to California from thirty days to less than ten. It was a very efficient service during its period of operation, carrying 35,000 pieces of mail over 65,000 miles (104,000 kilometers) and only losing one sack. Riders of the Pony Express were young, averaging just nineteen years of age. Horses used

on the route were changed every 15 miles (24 kilometers) at one of 190 relay stations. The original charge for mail delivery was ten dollars an ounce (28 grams), later reduced to one dollar an ounce. The Pony Express was the creation of a private company, Russell, Majors and Waddell. They lost over twenty thousand dollars on the service and were forced to declare bankruptcy. With the development of the telegraph, the Pony Express was unable to compete, and after just nineteen months of operation, the service was discontinued.

Wild Horses

The wild horses of the world have much different lives than domesticated breeds. In the wild, traveling in herds, horses, like many other animals, separate into groups. A stallion will gather a harem of mares to travel with him. A dominant stallion can have up to ten mares in his harem. Within that group, a lead mare develops and the others follow her. When a mare is ready to foal, she isolates herself in as remote an area as possible. After she gives birth and as

When horses are allowed to run free, they take full advantage of the opportunity, as is evident in this photo of a playful Thoroughbred.

Many of the islands around Great Britain have their own indigenous ponies, such as the Highland and the Shetland, which are able to manage the harshest of climates. Another island with a locally bred pony is Wales, where this Welsh Pony was foaled.

soon as her foal is able to move freely, the mare reunites with her herd for protection.

The most significant problems faced by wild horses are that they must feed and fend for themselves. They are particularly endangered by droughts. While other wild animals can survive eating bushes and shrubs, horses are more susceptible because of their need for grass, which suffers in a drought. A related problem faced by wild horses, and many other wild animals, is the size of their herd. When their numbers become too plentiful, the herd may not find enough food for all its members, or they may spread into areas where they are not wanted, either to be hunted or captured.

The great wild horse of America is the Mustang, which became its own breed in the sixteenth and seventeenth centuries. Horses set loose by Spanish settlers in Mexico formed herds along with stray horses. The Mustang is not as large as most warm-blooded breeds, ranging in height from 13 to 15 hands, but they are known for their speed and sturdiness. They roamed western America in large numbers for centuries. The herds were nearly wiped out in the twentieth century as Mustangs were hunted for their meat while the lands they roamed were

There is no secret so close as that between a rider and his horse."

—R. S. SURTEES

"Something like living occurs, a movement Out of the dream into its codification."

—JOHN ASHBERY,
Self-Portrait in a Convex Mirror

cleared for sheep and livestock. The hunting has since been stopped, as the Mustangs are now under government protection.

The wild horses of Australia are known as Brumbies. Like all other wild horses in the world today, they are "feral," meaning they have gone back into a wild state after the predecessors of their breed had been domesticated. Many Australian horses were used in wars early in the twentieth century. When there was no more military use for them, many were turned loose, eventually breeding with horses in the wild. A large breed developed which now lives in a protected area of a national park.

Most of the other wild breeds that still survive in the world live on barren, lightly populated islands. These include the Assateague Ponies, which live off the coast of Virginia in the United States. The island of Assateague was separated from the mainland during the 1930s. The Assateague Ponies are descendants of original Spanish imports to North America. Similar to the Mustang's history in Mexico, the Assateague are made up of horses which either strayed from their homes or were abandoned.

There are some breeds raised in a semi-wild state, usually not facing the dangers of totally wild horses. Among these breeds are the ancient Icelandic Horse, which is hardy enough to stay out of doors all year in its native country's harsh climate. The Icelandic Horse is actually a pony, standing between 12 and 14 hands. Vikings brought their Norwegian horses to Iceland in the ninth and tenth centuries, and the breed has remained pure for over a millennium. Also semi-wild is the Sable Island Pony, of Nova Scotia, Canada. This breed apparently originated from a herd of horses brought to the barren Sable Island in the eighteenth century.

Another breed which was previously wild currently exists only as domesticated. John Bell, a Scottish doctor, spotted a herd of wild horses in the mountains of Mongolia in the eighteenth century. In the nineteenth century, a Polish

"O, for a horse
with wings!"

—WILLIAM SHAKESPEARE,

Cymbeline

These wild Camargue horses graze in a deserted area of southeastern France. Many of the remaining wild horses in the world live on barren or deserted islands like Sable Island in eastern Canada or Assateague Island, off the coast of Virginia.

At one time Mustangs such as these in Nevada roamed by the millions through western North America. Though their numbers have been greatly reduced, those that remain are now under government protection.

colonel named N. M. Przewalski, also discovered a wild herd in Mongolia. The breed became known as the Mongolian Wild Horse, or, after the colonel who discovered them, Przewalski's Horse. Further research revealed these horses to be the lone surviving equine breed from the pre–Ice Age. Prehistoric cave paintings found in France bear a great resemblance to the Przewalski, which has a distinctive dun coat with a black mane. Unrefined by crosses with other breeds, its primitiveness is evident in its appearance, as its head looks more like that of an ass or donkey than most other horses.

Further studies indicate that in ancient times, the Przewalski used to roam through Europe and Asia in numbers estimated at around twenty thousand. By the time Dr. Bell and Colonel Przewalski discovered them, they had long since been driven back into the mountains of China and Asia. In the twentieth century the Przewalski began to die out, mostly as a result of weakened migration patterns. By 1945, there were only thirty-one individuals remaining. Through careful planning, their numbers have since grown more than tenfold, though they have become extinct in the wild. The breed now exists only in zoos and in a few privately owned stables, yet there is hope that in the future they can be reintroduced into their native wild habitat.

"My days have been so
wondrous free
The little birds that fly
With careless ease from
tree to tree,
Were but as bless'd as I."
—Thomas Parnell, *Song*

The sport of polo can be traced back nearly two thousand years. The expense of maintaining a large stable of horses necessary for the game has made it a sport played primarily, though not exclusively, by the wealthy. Here, a game takes place on a field in the posh Swiss resort of Saint Moritz.

Polo

Polo's history can be traced back about two thousand years to Tibet. Soon after it spread into Persia, and by the year 1000 a version of the game was being played in China and Japan. Polo was also played in India, where, in the nineteenth century, ruling British forces took up the game from the locals. Soon polo was brought back to England, and it quickly became a game of the British royalty and aristocracy.

Polo came to America as well, where one of its early exponents was a young George S. Patton, originally a cavalry officer. Patton considered the rugged nature of the sport good preparation for soldiers. The sport was popular with other Americans, too. In the 1920s, games played on the long since paved over open fields of New York's Long Island drew crowds in excess of 40,000. They came to watch the most famous of all polo players, Tommy Hitchcock, who dominated the sport in the 1920s and 1930s before he died in a plane crash in service during World War II.

Polo became a game of the wealthy by necessity. Simply keeping the stable of horses needed to play the game is a considerable expense, with the average Polo Pony today costing about $50,000. Most often a wealthy benefactor picks up the cost and also plays on the team, though usually in a minor role. He then hires other players, the best of whom are handsomely paid.

While other breeds are used for playing polo, the Polo Pony is an established type, though not a specific, standardized breed. It is also technically not a pony, although originally it evolved from a crossing of British ponies with small thoroughbreds. More recently, larger thoroughbreds have been crossed with Polo Ponies to produce a bigger, tougher, and faster horse. Most recent Polo Pony breeding has been centered in Argentina, where the sport is very popular and where its international team has been dominant in world competition since the 1930s. Though an old rule in the sport limiting the height of competing horses was abolished early in the twentieth century, the Polo Pony is still not that large—it is generally about 15 hands high.

The great sixteenth-
century artist Albrecht
Dürer rendered this
seemingly simple
portrait, entitled
Cavaliere, of a soldier
astride his war horse.

Dressage, Show Jumping, and the Olympics

Horse shows are popular events around the world, drawing particularly large crowds throughout Europe and America. Horse shows often feature a particular breed, or a particular discipline. The most dramatic event is show jumping, which often produces tense and exciting action as horses leap through a difficult obstacle course while running against a time standard. A second part of many horse shows, or often a separate event, is dressage. This discipline requires precise steps and other movements and even non-movements which display riders' control of their mounts. Both obstacle jumping and dressage are derived from nineteenth-century cavalry drills used to train and test the quality of horses used by the military.

A third part of some horse shows, or "equestrian events," is a cross-country run over obstacles which are much more difficult than those in show jumping. The course includes water jumps, sharp turns, and uneven terrain. The cross-country run requires a horse with speed, stamina, and courage.

Horses were a part of the original Olympics in Greece as far back as 680 B.C. Competitions involving horses then were limited to races, never a part of the modern Olympics. Horses were reintroduced into the Olympics in 1900 in Paris. Equestrian events that year consisted of a high jump and a long jump—both discontinued after that year—and obstacle course jumping, which has remained a major part of the Olympics.

Most of the other current Olympic equestrian events were added to the games in 1912 in Stockholm. These included dressage and the three-day event. Team competitions, which utilized the scores of all members of a country,

The Royal Canadian Mounted Police patrolled the vast open spaces of Canada's western provinces on horseback beginning in the middle of the nineteenth century. Today, horses are used only for ceremonial activities such as those pictured here.

Equestrian competition has been a part of the Olympics since 1900. Here, in the dressage competition from the 1996 Olympics in Atlanta, Mr. Guenta Seidel of the United States takes his mount Graf George through specified paces. Note the special saddle which allows the rider to sit more upright.

Show jumping is the most crowd-pleasing of all equestrian events, whether in a horse show or in the Olympics. Here, from the 1996 Atlanta Olympics, Extreme—the mount of Leslie Howard of the United States—attempts to clear an obstacle while racing against the clock.

were also added for some events in 1912. Team dressage was added in 1928. Unfortunately, dressage requires subjective judging, and like other such Olympic events—boxing, gymnastics, and figure skating, for instance—the history of dressage in the Olympics includes several instances of overt nationalism in the scoring of some judges.

In keeping with the military background of most equestrian events, all Olympic riders through the games of 1948 were required to be commissioned officers in their country, and they competed in the events in uniform.

A rider from Sweden was once disqualified when it was determined that he had not received a commission. The only exception to this rule was in 1920 in Antwerp, when a new discipline was added, figure riding. The only riders allowed to compete in this event were non-commissioned officers. Figure riding was dropped after its single Olympic appearance in 1920, never to return. In 1952 the rules of Olympic Equestrian events were changed dramatically, as all military requirements were dropped. In the same year, women riders were allowed to compete against men, as they have, successfully, ever since.

FOLLOWING PAGE:
Amidst Colorado's stunning surroundings, some horses from the Bell Tower Ranch enjoy the clear skies of a sunny winter day.

When they had their portraits painted, great figures in history frequently preferred being on horseback, which gave them an authoritative and vibrant appearance. This was especially true of Napoleon, portrayed here in *Bonaparte Crossing the Alps*, by his court painter Jacques-Louis David.

Roping steers—like the one
seen here—are a major part
of every traveling rodeo,
still popular in Canada and
the western United States.

Pleasure riding in the great parks of
urban centers was well established
by the end of the nineteenth century.
Here, two fashionable Parisians gallop
along a bridle path in *Riders in the
Bois de Boulogne* by Auguste Renoir.

The horse remained a vital part of the world's military forces for nearly four thousand years. The importance of the horse in battle is evident in this work, *"La Pucelle"—Jeanne d'Arc Leads Her Army* by FRANCK CRAIG

Horse Racing: A History

In India and Greece, racing of horses was known to be prevalent from at least 1000 B.C., and possibly much earlier. Racing was a major part of Greece's ancient Olympics, beginning in the seventh century B.C. Originally, the competition was strictly for four-horse chariots. Later, races for horses with riders were added, as were competitions for two-horse chariots and boy riders. Twelve-lap races were run in a hippodrome which had a length of approximately 1,000 feet (300 meters). The importance of these ancient Olympic events was so great that the winners were welcomed as heroes when they returned to their home cities.

Racing in Rome became very popular thanks to the patronage and participation of several emperors, most prominently Caligula, Nero, and Domitian. The very elaborate races of Rome, which were limited to chariot teams, were quite a spectacle, with the legs of the competing horses adorned with ornaments of ribbons and fronds. In Rome's Circus Maximus, as many as one hundred races were run in a single day.

Following the fall of the Roman Empire and the onset of the dark ages, horse racing could still be found in Europe, but generally it was not well organized and was merely a casual public or royal amusement. In the middle ages, many countries in Europe had large festival holidays which featured horse races among other events.

The next major development in horse racing history was the creation of the Thoroughbred.

One of the characteristics of the horse which has added to its appeal is its wide array and combinations of colors. Notice those of this show horse, Breezette, a light chestnut with a flowing blond mane.

In the seventeenth century, several members of Britain's royalty and nobility, along with the managers of their studs, established a breed designed for racing. Imported Arabian horses were crossed with the most prized English mares, which were derived from other breeds including Barbs. The original Arabian stallion was captured by Captain Byerley, a British officer, at Buda, in Hungary, which was then under Turkish control. Named the Byerley Turk, this stallion became one of three Thoroughbred foundation sires. The second was the Darley Arabian, imported from Syria by a Mr. Darley, a Yorkshire breeder. The third stallion was the Godolphin Arabian, also origi-nally from Syria, which was acquired for stud duty by the Earl of Godolphin.

These three original sires produced the four principal Thoroughbred lines. The Byerley Turk survived through his descendant Herod, foaled in 1758, and Herod's son, Highflyer; the Godolphin Arabian through the sire Matchem, foaled in 1748; and the Darley Arabian survived through the sire Eclipse, from 1764. Of these three, the Herod line has diminished dramatically in importance, as has the Matchem line, though it did produce the most famous Thoroughbred of the twentieth century, Man O' War. Of much greater importance today is the Eclipse line.

This stylized work by Théodore Géricault is en-titled *Horse Race at Epsom, 1821*. Horse racing at Epsom in England goes back to the eighteenth century and remains among the best in the world. Notice the upright riding styles of the jockeys, a style which was abandoned by the end of the nineteenth century following the suc-cess in England of the Ameri-can jockey Todd Sloane.

In the United States, the central Atlantic region of Maryland and Virginia remains one of the country's most active horse breeding areas. This chestnut is roaming through the fields of Maryland's Evergreen Stables.

It is responsible for all United States Triple Crown winners except for Man O' War's son War Admiral, as well as the most recent English Triple Crown winner (and prolific sire), Nijinsky II.

Through selective breeding, the size and speed of the newly created Thoroughbred increased through the eighteenth and nineteenth centuries. In the eighteenth century, a Thoroughbred that stood 15 hands high was exceptional. A century later, that height was common. As the Thoroughbred's speed increased, the distances of horse races, which were usually from 4 to 6 miles (6.5 x 9.5 kilometers), were shortened considerably to 3 miles (about 5 kilometers) and under. This allowed the breed to display its speed rather than its stamina. Horses became more precocious as well, racing at much younger ages.

During the eighteenth century, new and larger racecourses opened in England, including Doncaster, Newmarket, Epsom, and Ascot, all of which remain major racing centers today. Large racecourses were also opened in France, near Paris, including Longchamp, opened in 1837 and still the most important course in France, and Chantilly, which opened in 1834 and remained a racing center until the 1990s. Major races were established, such as the Derby and the Oaks, which remain the most important races today and which have been reproduced in every other racing country. Reminiscent of the large-scale festivals from in the middle ages, certain major race days attracted huge crowds and became traditional, festive days. There was Gold Cup Day at Ascot, Derby Day at Epsom, and Grand Prix Day at Longchamp. Eventually every country and almost every racecourse developed a schedule in which one day of the season was more significant than all others, a pattern which continues in horse racing today.

In the eighteenth century, national rules and regulations were established in Great Britain for the first time with the founding of the first Jockey Club, which was given power to watch over the sport. Official records were first kept, names of horses began to be registered, and pedigrees were listed in studbooks. (This was well after the foundation breeding of the Thoroughbred was established; the original pedigree records of the founding sires had been kept and preserved privately.)

The riding of racehorses became an established profession at this time, too. Previously, the owner might ride the horse himself, put a friend in the saddle, or, if light weight was needed, give the ride to a lad from the stable. Racing "silks" worn by jockeys became registered, with each owner having distinct colors. This tradition continues in Thoroughbred racing, though in Standardbred racing, the horse's driver, not the owner's, colors are used.

Horse Racing Around the World

American racing had started before the 1776 Revolution, and, spearheaded by Thoroughbred imports from England, continued to prosper throughout the nineteenth century. After America's Civil War, many American states outlawed racing at various times, only to bring it back later. These changes in the law continued well into the twentieth century, disturbing major racing in New York and California, among other places.

Early in the twentieth century, the overall quality of American Thoroughbreds was not up to the level of the French Thoroughbreds, which in turn were quite a bit below the quality of the English Thoroughbreds. These levels would remain so until after World War II, when the expensive importation of prolific and successful sires by American breeders changed the racing industry.

Though the American horses at the end of the nineteenth century were of a lower quality, the jockeys were superior to their European counterparts. These included such famous riders as Snapper Garrison and Isaac Murphy. In 1897 another successful American jockey, Todd Sloane, rode in England and achieved great success with a different riding style. While British riders stood high in the saddle with a straight back, Sloane crouched down, his back parallel to the horse's back. He also moved forward on the horse, riding nearly on the horse's neck. Sloane's style was aerodynamically superior to the old style and seemed to give better encouragement to the horse than the upright seat with the straight back. English traditionalists were outraged at the new style, describing its appearance as that of "a monkey on a stick." But soon all jockeys copied Sloane's successful style, though even today riders of Europe tend to sit more upright in the saddle than do American jockeys.

In Russia in the nineteenth century, harness racing, conducted in the winter months, grew in popularity. A major breed was developed, the Orlov Trotter, named after a Russian count. He crossed Arabian stallions with heavy Friesian horses to produce a breed of fast, elegant trotters. Harness racing became very popular in the United States also; unlike the Russian trotters, the American trotting breed, the Standardbred, descended from Thoroughbreds. When matched against the Orlov Trotters, the Standardbreds proved superior. By the middle of the nineteenth century, Standardbreds proved the higher quality of their Thoroughbred bloodlines by beating the best trotters of Europe as well. The Standardbred became the dominant breed for trotting and also for pacing. For over a century, the speed of the Standardbred has been continually upgraded through succeeding generations.

One reason the Standardbred has improved more noticeably in the twentieth century than has the Thoroughbred is that artificial insemination has been allowed. The procedure is still banned from Thoroughbred breeding, but its use with Standardbreds has permitted top stallions to sire many more foals a year than top Thoroughbred stallions. This has allowed the best Standardbred bloodlines to become more prevalent. The prohibition of artificial insemination in Thoroughbred breeding is predominantly for economic reasons, as its absence makes each mating of a top stallion a more scarce commodity.

For a very long time, horse racing and gambling have been basically inseparable. It has been a constant challenge for racing authorities to keep racing honest and to preclude the dishonest from participating. Scandals have been a part of racing for centuries, as the desire to get easy money has never lacked for appeal. The surest way to get an unfair advantage has always been to stop a horse from winning, either through bad shoeing or other means which prohibit a horse from running its best race. More complicated is getting a horse to run beyond its normal capabilities, usually with either an illegal chemical stimulant or some sort of illegal prod. These and other dishonest

Horses training on the Curragh, County Kildare, Ireland.

practices continue to be threats to the sport, though thanks to video tapes and laboratory testing, they are easier to detect than ever before. In any case, horse racing and gambling must coexist, since racing in most countries relies on a percentage of the money wagered, known as the "handle," for its revenue. Without betting there would be no money for purses, which would mean no money to pay jockeys, trainers, or anyone else involved in horse racing. The value of racehorses too would drop dramatically.

Thoroughbred racing takes place today in most countries of the world. The most important racing locations are now Japan, the United States, England, France, Australia, and Hong Kong. Many other countries have important racing industries as well, including Canada, Germany, Italy, Argentina, Brazil, and New Zealand. Most horse racing countries today follow the English tradition of running all their races over grass courses. The main exceptions are in North America and South America, which

run predominantly over dirt courses. Distances of races have continually been shortened, especially in the United States, where there is a very heavy emphasis on speed. Most American breeding of Thoroughbreds is geared to produce fast, precocious horses, and even high quality horses with stamina but not much speed are less desired and are usually exported.

Perhaps the most successful horse racing in the world today takes place in Japan, which had virtually no racing industry up until World War II. But after large, organized expenditures beginning in the 1950s, the sport has grown tremendously. Japanese breeders spent huge sums to bring in the best Thoroughbred bloodlines, and the quality of the Japanese Thoroughbred is now very high. Horse racing is also exceedingly successful in Hong Kong. The amount of money bet on each racecourse in both Japan and Hong Kong is in the hundreds of millions of dollars daily, totals which dwarf the betting handles of courses in Europe and America. As a result, the purses offered in

While stallions are always separated on a stud farm because of their potential aggression, mares are usually allowed to remain in the same field, as are these two Arabian mares on a farm in the state of Washington.

Japan and Hong Kong are much larger as well. Racing in Japan and Hong Kong is very restricted, however. For a long time in Japan, only horses bred in the country were allowed to race. Later, races were restricted to horses with Japanese owners. Very few races are offered for nonresident owners. These types of barriers do not exist in other major racing countries.

Australian racing is among the most popular in the world. Huge crowds attend the major racecourses on a regular basis, and, as in Asia, betting is very heavy. Melbourne Cup Day, held the first Tuesday in November, is a major event throughout Australia, in the manner of the large racing days and festivals of the past in Europe. In its own country, the Melbourne Cup draws at least as much attention as the Epsom Derby draws in England or the Kentucky Derby draws in America. Australian Thoroughbred breeding has been improved in recent times because quarantine restrictions for horses imported into the country have been made less stringent. Many more well-bred horses have entered the country, and, with the reversal of seasons in

the northern and southern hemispheres, some popular Thoroughbred stallions can now be shipped from North America or Europe, where they can be bred from September through January, in the southern hemisphere's spring and summer.

European racing has been dominated for many years by the Maktoums, a family of sheiks from the United Arab Emirates. Apparent possessors of unlimited resources, the Maktoums have bought up virtually all of the available fashionable Thoroughbred bloodlines since the 1980s and have won all of the major races of Europe, concentrating particularly on England's races. In addition, the Maktoums have expanded their racing and breeding operations to the United States and Australia. They also have established racing in their home city of Dubai. The Maktoums' wealth has allowed them to create the world's richest horse race, normally run in the spring at the Dubai racecourse. Run over a dirt track, the race attracts the world's best horses, whose transportation expenses to Dubai are paid by the sheiks.

A Thoughbred colt romps through a field in County Kildare, Ireland.

Coursing was a hunt in which the hounds chased their game by sight rather than scent. The elaborate nature of these events is portrayed in this nineteenth-century work by William and Henry Barraud, *The Wiltshire Great Coursing Meeting, Held at Amesbury, With Stonehenge Beyond.*

Horses were a part of the most significant steps in the development of the American West, including the construction of railroads and the transportation of settlers. Horses, both wild and domesticated, continue to roam the West, including this one seen in a snowy Colorado field.

Though the harsh winters of Great Britain produce a hardy pony, the rainy springs result in fertile grounds that help the development of new foals, such as this Welsh Pony seen romping with its mother.

Simone Martini was Siena's leading painter
in the fourteenth century. His portrait of
Guidoriccio da Fogliano, taking part in the siege
of an enemy stronghold, shows that horses
of the time wore the same robes as their rider.

"Along a parabola
life like a rocket flies,
Mainly in darkness,
now and then
on a rainbow."

—ANDREI VOZNESENSKI,
Parabolic Ballad

CHAPTER THREE

A WORLD OF HORSES

The American Saddle-bred, seen here trotting across the Rainbow Ranch in Colorado, is a breed developed originally in America's south during the nine-teenth century. It is known for its distinc-tive high-stepping gait.

American Saddlebred

The American Saddlebred was developed in the American South during the nineteenth century and was originally known as the Kentucky Saddler. Tracing to the old Narra-gansett Pacer and the Canadian Pacer, the American Saddlebred was refined through crosses with the Thoroughbred and the Morgan, which developed its speed and movement. The breed has legs that are unusually light, and their hooves are allowed to grow long. The American Saddle-bred is now a very popular show horse most known for its fancy gaits, both at slow and fast speeds. It is also well known for its high-stepping action.

Andalusian

The Andalusian—a direct descendant of the Spanish Horse—is one of the oldest breeds in existence. It is named for the region in which the breed was developed, the fertile lands of southwest Spain. The Carthusian Monks of the region are more famous for creating Chartreuse liqueur, but they were also responsible for pre-serving the Andalusian breed. Today the center of Andalusian breeding remains in southwestern Spain in Jerez de la Frontera.

Unlike most warm-blooded breeds, the Andalu-sian is not known for its speed, though it is agile and athletic. Its physical appearance is quite distinctive, with a short but quite muscular neck, very sturdy legs, and long, thick hair on its tail and mane.

The Andalusian, such as the one seen here in a playful mood, is, like the equally well balanced Lipizanner, a direct descendant of the versatile Spanish Horse. The breed was developed in the lush lands of southern Spain, which is still the center of Andalusian breeding.

There are other horses with spotted coats but the Appaloosa is clearly the best known and most common. Its coloring has five established patterns, designations which differentiate the original coat, the size of the spots, and the pattern of the spots. One of these is called blanket, in which the hips are covered in white, often with dark spots. Another is called marble, which is dark hair around the outside of the body with white in the middle. A third pattern is called leopard, a white coat with dark spots. The fourth pattern, called snowflake, has most of the spotting over the hips. And the final spotting pattern is called frost, which is a dark coat with white markings.

The Arabian breed was developed about two thousand years ago, and the expansion of the Muslim Empire more than a thousand years ago spread the Arabian breed throughout much of Europe and Asia.

The Appaloosa was derived from Spanish horses of western North America. Its famous spots come in five different patterns. The white coat with dark spots on this Appaloosa, photographed on a winter day in Colorado, is termed the leopard pattern.

Appaloosa

Now a popular horse to ride but also used in racing, the Appaloosa was named for the Palouse River Valley in western North America. The breed's famous spotted coat was developed in the eighteenth century by the Nez Percé Indians of the American northwest. Utilizing mostly spotted horses of Spanish stock, the Nez Percé raised the Appaloosa into a strong and agile though not overly large working breed. Native Americans utilized the horse for buffalo hunting, which enabled the tribe to better expand its food supply.

In the late nineteenth century, the Appaloosa nearly became extinct during the wars between the United States and Native American tribes. However, the breed not only has revived in the twentieth century, it has flourished and become the third-largest equine breed in the world.

Arabian

One of the oldest breeds in the world, the Arabian's heritage goes back about two thousand years. All Thoroughbreds can be traced to the Arabian, and, like its descendant, the Arabian is today raced in competition, though it lacks the Thoroughbred's speed. The bloodlines of the Arabian breed have been meticulously preserved in international studbooks, maintained today by the World Arabian Horse Organization.

Though it is not as fast as other breeds, and at between 14 and 15 hands it is smaller and less powerful, the Arabian is perhaps the breed most admired for its beauty and appearance, and is well known for stamina and soundness under saddle. Arabian auctions are often quite elaborate and more glamorous presentations than are other horse sales. The most sought after Arabians garner huge bids at these auctions.

Ardennais horses are not as tall as most other draft horses but, as this photograph of the breed shows, they have very powerful bodies, especially through the shoulders and neck. The legs are also particularly sturdy.

Ardennais

The Ardennais derives from an ancient horse from northwestern France and Belgium. In the nineteenth century, the breed was refined through crossings with another large breed, the Belgian. A second type of Ardennais was created in the nineteenth century through crosses with Arabians and Thoroughbreds. This produced a smaller, more agile Ardennais used for lighter burdens. This lighter breed is now not nearly as common as the larger Ardennais.

The Ardennais' traditional use has been on the farms of the French and Belgian Ardennes region. At under 16 hands, it is one of the shorter draft horses, but it is also quite powerful. It has a very wide body with extremely sturdy legs which are feathered unusually heavily.

Belgian Heavy Draft

The Belgian is also known as the Brabant, a region in Belgium which, in medieval times, was one of the most prosperous duchies in Europe. The great power of the Belgian horse was utilized throughout the middle ages by the Brabant military. The breed itself goes back much further, and is possibly a direct descendant of the ancient Forest Horse. The Belgian's strength made it an influence sought after throughout Europe. The breeders of Ardennais, Boulonnais, and Clydesdales, among others, used the Belgian's bloodlines to increase the size and power of their breeds.

The coat of the Belgian was refined in the nineteenth century, and the breed today is most known for its chestnut roan color. Among all draft horses, the Belgian is second in size to the Shire, weighing from 1,700 to 2,200 pounds (818 to 1,010 kilograms). Most Belgians looks less like draft horses than any other heavy breed. Though its frame is certainly powerful and heavily muscled, its legs often give an appearance of length not evident in other draft horses.

The large and very powerful Belgian is one of the most influential of all heavy breeds. Breeders of other draft horses have used crosses with the Belgian to increase the strength of other breeds.

The Boulonnais breed, from France, developed its gray coat through crosses with the Arabian, which also increased its mobility. This Boulonnais possesses the breed's typically short but powerful cannon bones.

Breeders in northwestern France crossed their local large horses with other heavier breeds to produce the Breton. It is one of the better moving draft horses, known for its fine trotting action.

Boulonnais

A cold-blooded horse of northwest France, the Boulonnais was developed nearly two thousand years ago from a crossing of the local large horses with the more agile horses brought to the region by the controlling Roman Empire. Through the subsequent centuries, the Boulonnais was further developed by crosses with heavier breeds as well as with Spanish horses. A very popular breed today, the Boulonnais shows an Arabian influence both in its nimbleness and in its gray color. The Boulonnais' legs are typically muscular for a heavy draft horse, with the distinctive feature of very short cannon bones. Standing between 15 and 17 hands, the Boulonnais is still used for heavy agricultural hauling. In the days before mechanization, it was used to carry fish from the dock to market.

Breton

The Breton comes from the distinctive region of northwestern France. The Breton was crossed with several other cold-blooded breeds, including the Boulonnais, the Percheron, and the Ardennais. These produced a breed of great strength known also for its fine trotting action. A typical draft horse, the Breton is quite compact, with very sturdy legs, hard hooves, and powerful neck and shoulders. It is one of the shorter cold-blooded breeds, with some members less than 16 hands. The Breton's primary utilization has been in farm work.

Cleveland Bay

An influential breed of the past which is now not as plentiful, the Cleveland Bay is a British breed dating from the middle ages. Crosses of horses from Cleveland, in northern England, with Spanish horses produced a sturdy breed of good mobility. The Cleveland Bay is especially noted for its jumping ability, a trait it has passed on to other breeds, including the Hunter. Since the eighteenth century, the Cleveland Bay has been the horse of choice for transporting England's royal family.

The very agile Cleveland Bay has been the carriage horse of England's royal family for centuries. Here a team of Cleveland Bays transports a royal carriage in a ceremony at Windsor.

Clydesdale

The Clydesdale breed goes back to eighteenth-century Scotland. Breeders in that area imported the heavier draft horses from Flanders to cross with their own smaller and less powerful cold-bloods. They succeeded in producing a bigger breed, as mature Clydesdales weigh between 1,600 and 1,900 pounds (760 to 900 kilograms).

By the end of the nineteenth century, the Clydesdale was recognized as unique. Named for the valley around Scotland's Clyde River, it quickly became popular in North America and soon was

exported to most regions of the world. The breed is well known for its good movement, with a distinctive high-stepping action which has added greatly to its popularity.

The Clydesdale was originally developed for heavy agricultural work but, because of its international popularity, it has been used for many other purposes. Early in the twentieth century, the American brewery Anheuser-Busch delivered their beer in huge wagons pulled by eight horses in harness. Eventually the brewery, based in St. Louis, Missouri, acquired Clydesdales for their wagons. Anheuser-Busch began breeding its own stock, and in the process produced several champions of the breed. Long after beer was no longer delivered by horse-drawn wagon, the Clydesdales remained a powerful advertising symbol for the brewery. Teams of their horses usually accompany promotional tours, which have made the Clydesdales one of the most recognized and admired of all breeds. The Anheuser-Busch Clydesdale stables in St. Louis have been designated by the United States Government a historic national landmark.

The nimbleness of the large Clydesdales has made them a popular attraction at fairs and other public events. Here a team of Clydesdales performs at a show in Calgary, Alberta, Canada, in 1994.

Cob

Not a breed with specific standards, the Cob is a very versatile horse. Many Cobs can both pull a harness and be ridden under saddle. In addition, a Cob can display a wide variety of gaits when performing in show events. When appearing in public, the Cob's mane is frequently cut very short, emphasizing its muscular neck. Though not of clearly defined heritage, most Cobs have been influenced by a wide variety of breeds. These usually include heavy draft horses from Ireland as well as the much more nimble Welsh Cob, known for its trotting, and the Cleveland Bay, known for its jumping.

Exmoor

The Exmoor Pony is a very ancient breed, apparently a direct descendant of an original Equus subspecies of northwestern Europe which predates both the Arabian and the Barb. The Exmoor comes from the harsh, high moorland of Somerset and Devonshire, England. A hilly wasteland, this part of England is isolated and desolate, and the Exmoor pony that adapted to this region is robust and resistant to bad weather.

The Exmoor is strong enough to haul large loads yet still maintains good mobility. The breed is respected for its jumping ability. Like many equines comfortable in cold climates, the Exmoor has long nasal passages which warms the air that is inhaled. Like many ponies, the breed has short, sturdy legs and hard hooves. In contrast to other ponies or any other current equine breed, however, is their primitive jaw formation, which includes an extra molar no other breed possesses.

Seen here are Exmoor mares with their new foals. Notice the lack of
refinement in the head of the Exmoor Pony, one of the oldest breeds
in existence. Its jaw formation is different from all other equines,
and its mouth includes an extra molar possessed by no other breed.

Among the heavy breeds, the Friesian is less known for its strength than for its mobility, as displayed here. Note too the breed's distinctive black coat and its hard, heavily feathered hooves.

Friesian

A cold-blooded breed of ancient origin, the Friesian comes from the northern coast of Holland, known as Friesland. A major influence through crosses with several breeds of Great Britain, the Friesian is noted for its distinctive black coat. Its hooves are very hard and sound, and covered by heavy feathering, and its mane is one of the longest and fullest of any breed. The Friesian is not noted for its strength but rather its good movement, particularly in harness, though also under saddle. Its mobility and good temperament have made it a useful war-horse in the past, and the Friesian was employed by local knights riding to the Crusades. Early in the twentieth century, the breed was very close to extinction, with at one point as few as three surviving stallions. But careful planning resuscitated the Friesian and it is again a thriving breed.

Hackney Horse

Not to be confused with the Hackney Pony, the Hackney Horse was developed in England in the nineteenth century. The breed was created from the Norfolk and Yorkshire Roadsters, two descendants of Thoroughbreds that became noted for trotting at high speeds and with heavy burdens. The Hackney became a reputable carriage horse in England, and today it is one of the world's most popular harness horses in show rings. Hackneys are almost uniform in height, between 15 and 16 hands. They are not heavily muscled but are well known for a fluid stride, with their front legs moving upward in an unusually elevated action.

Hackney Pony

Like the Hackney Horse, the Hackney Pony descends from Norfolk and Yorkshire Roadsters of the eighteenth century. In England in the nineteenth century, crosses of the Hackney with Pony bloodlines created the new, distinct breed. Used strictly under harness, the Hackney Pony has a naturally elevated stride which makes it a favorite in the show ring. It is an average-size pony, with members of the breed varying from 12 to 14 hands. Most notable is the upright way the breed holds its head, much more so than other ponies.

Hanoverian

Europe's Great War Horse is thought to be the main ancestor of the Hanoverian, one of Germany's most popular warmblood breeds. Arab, Thoroughbred, and Trakehner blood were used to refine and develop the breed and it is now popular both as a pleasure horse and as the mount of serious equestrians. The breed's historic home is in Lower Saxony, in northern Germany, the former Kingdom of Hanover where a flourishing horse-breeding industry has existed for four hundred years.

FOLLOWING PAGE: A Hanoverian gallops through a field at the Imperial Egyptian Stud. This is probably Germany's best-known and best-loved breed, descended from the Great War Horse with infusions of Arab and Thoroughbred into its bloodline.

The Hackney was derived from eighteenth-century English trotters, or "roadsters." Today they are very popular in show rings, pulling a harness with their high-stepping strides.

The Hunter is not a specific breed because different countries have different standards for them. But Hunters must have good athletic ability (as this one displays), stamina, courage, and an even disposition.

Highland

The Highland Pony can be traced back nearly ten thousand years to northern Scotland and the Scottish Islands, though the breed apparently stretches further to the pre–Ice Age in France. Today's Highland Pony is the product of crosses with several other, quite different breeds, including the Spanish Horse, the Clydesdale, the Arabian, and the Percheron. These crosses have increased the size, strength, and mobility of the Highland. It is now one of the tallest ponies, standing at between 14 and 15 hands. It is well known for its ability to haul heavy loads, though it is also used commonly under saddle. The Highland's most notable physical characteristic is its very powerful neck.

Hunter

The Hunter is a warm-blooded type, rather than a breed, because it has varying standards in different locations. As a result, Hunters range in height from 15 to 17 hands. Most Hunters have speed inherited from crosses with Thoroughbreds, and jumping ability, which comes from the influence of another breed, the Cleveland Bay. The Thoroughbred and the Cleveland Bay were originally crossed with Irish draft horses. This produced in the Hunter a horse of good athletic ability and movement yet which is not as high-strung nor as fragile as, for example, the Thoroughbred.

Breeders in the harsh northern islands of Scotland developed the Highland Pony through crosses with a wide array of large and small horses, producing a breed which is very powerful for its size. These Highland Ponies are seen during some unusually mild Scottish weather.

Lipizzaner

This Lipizanner displays the bright gray colors which have added to the breed's popularity. The Lipizanner was derived from the Spanish Horse in the sixteenth century, designed for the riding stables of the Viennese Court.

The Lipizzaner was developed in Slovenia in the sixteenth century by the Hapsburg Archduke, Charles II. In 1572 the Viennese Court founded the Spanish School, which taught horsemanship to members of the nobility, utilizing only "Spanish" horses. In 1580 the Archduke imported thirty-three Spanish horses (nine stallions and twenty-four mares) to produce a group of predominantly white horses for the royal stables of Vienna. The name of

Lipizzaner comes from the Slovenian stud where the breed was then developed.

The Lipizzaner, with its bright gray colors and elegance appearance, is today a striking and very popular show horse. It appears under both harness and saddle, though in most of its international public appearances it performs in unified groups while being ridden. The Lipizzaner stands between 15 and 16 hands and has a fairly sturdy look. It is as yet bred today in

Slovenia as well as in Austria (where it is still used for the Spanish School), Hungary, Rumania, and the Czech Republic.

Morgan

The foundation sire of the Morgan breed was named for its American owner, Justin Morgan. Foaled in the late eighteenth century in Massachusetts of unclear heritage, Justin Morgan was used by its owner for heavy hauling and farm work. It was also raced successfully both by harness and under saddle. The characteristics of the foundation sire are still evident in the breed, as the Morgan is known for its strength and stamina as well as its easy handling. These traits made the Morgan the horse of choice for the United States Cavalry. The Morgan is now a popular horse in show rings, with shoes often designed to give it an unnaturally elevated stride.

A Morgan and her foal romp through the countryside. All Morgans trace to an eighteenth-century foundation sire, Justin Morgan, known for both his speed and strength, traits still present in the breed.

Seen here is a Noriker, a breed developed in the Austrian Alps. Crosses with heavier breeds have increased its strength, and crosses with Spanish Horses have improved its movement.

Noriker

The Noriker is the heavy breed indigenous to the Austrian Alps. Monasteries of the region were helpful in establishing the breed in the sixteenth century. The Noriker was further advanced by crosses with other cold-blooded breeds, which increased its power, and with Spanish blood, which improved its movement and refined its physique. Today, the performance standards and the physical requirements of the Noriker breed are rigorously enforced.

Though not small, at between 16 and 17 hands, the Noriker cannot handle heavy loads. But it is a very efficient worker carrying light drafts. Because of its place of origin, the breed is resistant to bad weather. The Noriker is also easier to manage than most heavy breeds.

Oldenburg

Originally developed as a good strong carriage horse, the Oldenburg is now highly popular as a riding and driving horse, and represents one of the top lines in Germany. The Oldenburg is large, standing 16.3 hands high. It is bred in a small area near the region of Lower Saxony surrounding the city of Oldenburg. Originally from East Friesland, a part of Holland, its complex ancestry includes Andalusian and Barb, as well as Hanoverian and Thoroughbred lines.

Most lighter breeds are natural jumpers and will kick up their back legs to show their enthusiasm, as this Oldenburg does on a Maryland farm.

The tan or gold coat of the Palomino may be the most distinctive of all equines. Registered Palominos must conform to certain color standards which limit the amount of dark or white hair in the coat.

The powerful and mobile Percheron was developed by French breeders who crossed their local large horses with Arabians. This Percheron is one of many which have the gray coat that reflects the breed's Arabian influence.

Palomino

The actual term Palomino describes a color rather than a breed, as all Palominos have a distinctive gold or beige coat. Like so many North American–based horses, Palominos (and their distinct coloring) descend from the Spanish Horse. Today, registered Palominos must have one parent who is either a Quarter Horse, Arabian, or Thoroughbred. Each registered Palomino must also meet specific color guidelines, including limits on both dark hair and white markings. Because of the influences of different breeds, Palominos have a wider variance of size than most other breeds, ranging in height from 14 to 16 hands.

Percheron

The horse which was thought to be the largest of the species in the world was a Percheron, named Dr. Le Gear—21 hands high and weighing more than a ton and a half (1,360 kilograms). Most Percherons aren't nearly that big, standing between 16 and 18 hands, but the Percheron's size and strength are always evident. Originating in northern France, the large Percheron ancestors were refined over many centuries through crosses with Arabian blood. The current Percheron breed was established in the eighteenth century. Its Arabian crosses added to its mobility, as the Percheron's fluid stride differentiates it from other heavy breeds. The Arabian influence also produced a gray color in many Percherons, which has added to their popularity. The Percheron traditionally works on farms and provides transportation, as is typical of a heavy draft horse.

Pinto

Also known as the Paint Horse, the Pinto (a name derived from the Spanish *pintado*, meaning painted) traces its origins to the Spanish stock brought to the Americas in the sixteenth century. The coat of the Pinto features huge splashes or blotches of color. A predominantly white coat with dark blotches is referred to as Tobiano, while a mostly dark coat with white coverings in called Ovaro. The Pinto breed has a wide variety of sizes, though their height is a fairly uniform 15 to 16 hands.

Quarter Horse

Among the Quarter Horse's greatest assets is its versatility. Bred and raced for its speed, the Quarter Horse also has been used frequently on farms and ranches, with a special ability to work with cattle. The Quarter Horse is so named because of its high speed for a quarter-mile, a trait developed in the breed in America in the seventeenth century. The original American Quarter Horses were derived from both English and Spanish stock.

Though they do run up to a half-mile, a quarter-mile is now the distance which the breed usually runs when it is in competition. Quarter Horse racing is a large industry in the United States today, particularly popular in the areas where the breed was worked extensively on ranches, in the nation's southwest and west. To increase the speed of the Quarter Horse, much Thoroughbred blood has been added to the breed. The breed tends to be heavily muscled in the legs, a trait evident in racehorses that have quick speed rather than stamina.

The blotches or spots of the Pinto have a splashed-on look. This Pinto's predominantly white coat with dark splashes is known as Tobiano. A dark coat with light spots is called Ovaro coloring.

Quarter Horses continue to be used
extensively on American ranches
to tend to cattle and other animals.
Quarter Horse racing is quite popular in the same western regions.

Shires, seen here running through a field in North America's New England region, are probably the biggest and strongest of all equines. They often weigh over 2,500 pounds (1,200 kilograms) but they maintain good mobility acquired through earlier crossings with the Frenchman.

Shetland Pony

One of the oldest breeds of any size, the Shetland Pony's origins can be traced to at least 8000 B.C. Developed in the northernmost reaches of the United Kingdom, in Scotland's inhospitable Shetland Islands, it is possible that the Shetland descended from the original Tundra Horse of Siberia, hence its ability to withstand even the harshest of climates.

Despite its size (between 9.5 and 10.5 hands) the Shetland Pony is one of the most powerful of all equines. Its strength and toughness come from its very compact physique, including quite sturdy legs and very hard hooves. Through the centuries, it has been used for hauling heavy loads, such as carrying coal out of mines. The Shetland was used as well for transporting carriages over difficult terrain and through rough weather. The Shetland can be ridden under saddle, though—because of its short back—only by small children.

Shire

England's Shire was derived from the Old English Horse of medieval times. The current standard of the breed was established in the nineteenth century, when it was known as the English Cart Horse. The Shire's strength was improved through crosses with other heavy breeds, and its mobility was increased through crosses with the Friesian. Today the Shire is usually considered the strongest of all draft horses as well as the heaviest, often weighing over 2,500 pounds (about 1,200 kilograms). In weight-pulling exhibitions, pairs of Shires have pulled the equivalent of 50 tons (about 45,000 kilograms). Standing between 16 and 18 hands, the Shire, with very thick bone mass, has enormous strength in its legs. Its large lower legs are heavily feathered, making them hard to keep clean. This detracted from the Shire's popularity until dirt roads became much less prominent.

A Shetland Pony is shown with her new foal. A breed whose history goes back at least ten thousand years, the very sturdy Shetland Pony can ably withstand the harsh climate of its native island.

Standardbred

The term Standardbred was not at all meant to imply anything ordinary about this breed, but rather to indicate that approved registrants had been able to meet a high, established racing-time standard. All current Standardbreds are descendants of a Thoroughbred, specifically the eighteenth-century stallion Messenger. In the nineteenth century, the prolific stallion and dominant racer Hambletonian had a major and lasting influence on the breed.

Throughout much of the world today, the Standardbred is raced extensively under harness (though in some areas, namely France, also under saddle). Particularly popular in Sweden, France, Italy, New Zealand, Canada, and the United States, Standardbred racing, or, as it is better known, harness racing, enjoys popularity second only to the Thoroughbred among equines. Standardbreds race in two specific gaits: the trot, the style used exclusively in Europe, and the pace, more popular and more common in North America and New Zealand. In North America, most Standardbred races are run at 1 mile (1.6 kilometers), but elsewhere the distances are more varied.

Suffolk Punch

The Suffolk Punch is one of the better moving of all cold-blooded draft horses, and though it is the smallest of all heavy breeds it does not lack for strength. The breed is particularly noted for its trotting gait, which it probably inherited from Norfolk Roadsters, renowned for their trotting. The Suffolk Punch became a recognized breed late in the eighteenth century. All current members of the breed descend from one stallion, known as Thomas Crisp's Horse, foaled in 1768. A distinguishing feature of each Suffolk Punch is its distinctive chestnut color, developed through crosses with the large Flanders Horse. It is the only draft horse with consistent coloring.

The Suffolk Punch has small hooves for a draft horse. Its hindquarters and girth are unusually rounded, giving it an unathletic look which belies its capabilities. The breed has been an ideal horse for farm work, partly because its hooves are unfeathered. This allows the horse to work in dusty conditions too difficult for other heavy draft horses. The Suffolk Punch is known for a particularly hardy constitution and for its longevity. Most members of the breed are capable of working in the field

FOLLOWING PAGE:

"In solitude
  What happiness?
Who can enjoy
  alone,
Or all enjoying,
  what contentment
  find?"
  —*JOHN MILTON,*
  Paradise Lost

This photo of a Suffolk Punch shows why members of this breed have a reputation for being too round and fat. But their appearance belies their capabilities, as the Suffolk Punch is a powerful heavy horse well known for its good movement.

The horse racing
industry has made
the Thoroughbred
the most influential
equine breed today,
and the most valuable.
Some of the world's
most important Thor-
oughbred breeding
farms are in Lexing-
ton, Kentucky, inclu-
ding Calumet Farm,
shown here. Calumet
is famous for its
white fences and
Devil's Red outlines,
as well as for its
champion racehorses.

well past the age of twenty. They are able to survive and even thrive on a diet much more sparse than other large breeds, allowing the Suffolk Punch to be maintained less expensively than other draft horses.

Tennessee Walking Horse

A saddle horse of solid colors, the good-natured Tennessee Walking Horse dates from the eighteenth and nineteenth centuries. Standing between 15 and 16 hands, this breed weighs in the vicinity of 900 to 1,200 pounds (410 to 540 kilograms). Its unique pacing gait can be traced to the Narragansett Pacer. It picked up the distinctive walk (for which it was named) from its foundation sire, the Standardbred Black Allan. Other breeds that have mixed into the development of the Tennessee Walking Horse are the Thoroughbred, the Morgan, and the American Saddlebred.

Thoroughbred

The financial importance of the horse racing industry throughout the world has made the Thoroughbred the most valuable of all equines. At the top of the market, a few Thoroughbred stallions have been valued in excess of one hundred million dollars. The Thoroughbred is not only the most expensive horse in the world, it is, not coincidentally, the fastest. Centuries of developing the breed have produced Thoroughbreds without as much stamina as their ancestors, but with more speed. Many other breeds have been crossed with Thoroughbred blood to increase their quickness and refine their appearance.

The Thoroughbred's proportions are geared for speed, with long, lean legs and hindquarters which can become quite muscular. Champion Thoroughbreds have varied in size from 15 hands to over 17 hands. Two distinct difficulties of the Thoroughbred are its temperament and fragility. The Thoroughbred tends to be very high-strung and more difficult to handle than most other breeds. Also, the high speed asked of the Thoroughbred under saddle has produced numerous tragedies as a result of broken bones in the legs.

Always performing under saddle, the Tennessee Walking Horse has a distinctive gait, displayed here, which it inherited from its foundation sire, the Standardbred trotter Black Allan.

Developed in the thirteenth century for military use, the Trakehner is one of the best moving and soundest of all breeds. It is often seen in dressage and other equestrian events.

Behind the long hair is a Welsh Pony, which is one of three distinctive breeds of Welsh ponies. The original is the Welsh Mountain Pony, followed by the Welsh Pony, and finally the Welsh Pony of Cob Type, the most powerful of the three.

Trakehner

With its excellent conformation, athletic ability, and speed, the Trakehner is one of the world's most popular breeds in dressage and equestrian events. Its origins stretch to the thirteenth century when the breed was formed from the ancient bloodlines of the Tarpan. Developed by the Teutonic Knights in Prussia, the Trakehner breed was further advanced in the eighteenth century by the opening of the Trakehner Stud, which produced horses for the Prussian cavalry.

In subsequent centuries, the Trakehner has been influenced by outside bloodlines, specifically Arabians and Thoroughbreds, which have added speed and size to the breed. The Trakehner, like much of the horse population of Europe, was threatened by the destruction during World War II. But Trakehner breeders were able to move about five percent of them away from the hostilities and continue the breed after the war.

Welsh Ponies

There are three distinct breeds of Welsh ponies: the Welsh Pony, the Welsh Mountain Pony, and the Welsh Pony of Cob Type. The Welsh Mountain Pony is the original, having been in Wales before recorded history. It is the smallest of the three, with an average height of about 12 hands; the other two breeds are normally over 13 hands.

The Welsh Mountain Pony was crossed with other breeds, particularly Arabians and Thoroughbreds, to increase its speed and scope. It makes a striking appearance under both saddle and harness, and like other mountain or moorland breeds of Great Britain it is able to handle difficult terrain and harsh climates. The Welsh Pony's greater size and longer legs make it a better jumper than the Mountain Pony. The Welsh Pony of Cob Type has noticeably thicker legs and a much stronger neck. As a result, the Cob Type has been used more extensively for work—on farms as well as in Welsh mines—than have the other two Welsh pony breeds.

"Now I adore my life
With the Bird, the abiding Leaf,
With the Fish, the questing Snail,
And the Eye altering all;
And I dance with William Blake
For love, for Love's sake."

—THEODORE ROETHKE, *Once More, the Round*

Conclusion

How did the ancient world explain the existence of the horse and its very distinctive characteristics? Different cultures developed a variety of legends. For instance, according to Roman mythology, after the creation of the city of Athens Jupiter declared that the new city would be named after whichever god produced the most worthy object for the human race. The god Neptune then revealed his wondrous creation, the horse (he lost the contest, however, to Minerva's more peaceful offering of an olive tree).

The ancient myths offered explanations about the most striking quality of the horse—its speed. There are Greek legends, as well as some from other countries, that credit the wind for giving the horse its quickness. In certain myths, a god of wind was said to have taken the form of a stallion and impregnated mares, imbuing the foals with the wind's swiftness. Another widely held belief was that the horse's speed came via wings. Most of the celebrated of the ancient horses of legend were winged, including Pegasus, the very swift white horse of the god Apollo, and India's Surya, a horse described as possessing "falcon's wings." A Hindu legend has it that horses' wings were removed so that man would be able catch the animals and control them.

Ancient myths tell of fantastic creatures that were only part horse. These included the centaur, half man and half horse, well known from Greek fables. Most centaurs were savage, though one, Chiron, was described as a scholar and teacher of Achilles and Hercules. Another mixed species of legend is the unicorn. In some tales it is a gentle, peaceful symbol of innocence, with the body of a horse, the tail of a lion, and a distinctive horn sprouting from its forehead. In other versions, the unicorn is a very fierce beast, still part horse but also part deer, boar, and even elephant.

Amidst this background of astonishing legends, it is not surprising that certain cultures assumed horses possessed supernatural powers, both during and after life. The Saxons believed that the neighing of horses was prophetic. In Persia, a king was chosen by assembling the horses of all prospects for the throne. The owner of the horse that neighed first was named king. In a number of pagan countries, including Greece, Persia, and Assyria, horses were offered up in sacrifice to appease a god, most often a sun god or a sea god.

Today only remnants of such beliefs remain. Horseshoes are still occasionally hung on doors for luck or because they are thought to keep evil spirits away.

Their mythic and majestic nature as well as an unmistakable splendor explains why the horses of ancient kings and pharaohs were buried alongside their masters. Likewise, to this day, with quicker and easier means of transportation readily available, many people still enjoy riding or being pulled along by a horse, and millions more simply enjoy the company of a horse.

INDEX

128